For Fiona, who has loved me more than any one man deserved.

Introduction

1 My God, my God, why have you abandoned me? Why are you so far away when I groan for help? 2 Every day I call to you, my God, but you do not answer. Every night you hear my voice, but I find no relief.

I am no King David; I am as far from his situation as it is possible to be; living in a cold, windy northern hemisphere in the 21st century in relative peace and ease, working for a living and living in the good of promises that were prophecies when the great king wrote them.

I do, however, understand his cries in this song, but that's me getting ahead of myself.

Many people way more qualified than I am have written about depression, its medical roots and spiritual causes (D Martyn Lloyd Jones in his book, Spiritual Depression explores this great subject in some detail and the roots in the soul of man) and my purpose is not to reinvent the wheel or bring some ground breaking research to the world. There are studies ongoing this year linking depression to inflammation in the body that can act as a trigger to this hideous disease.

So why bother with yet another opinion on depression? Well as a Christian of 29 years and a pastor for 3 years I had read it all, heard most of it and been helped by none of it. In the church depression is a hot potato, we all know it exists but are not quite sure what to do with it; and when I say 'it' what we are speaking about is a living breathing person who is in desperate need of understanding, not a problem to fix or a nuisance to be ignored or hidden away.

If I can accomplish that for one person then all of this will have been worthwhile.

I read somewhere that you should write the book that you wish you could have read, it is with that thought in mind that I am offering my experience here.

Beginnings

1

For me, depression has always been a sign that my life is about to change direction. Everyone has different triggers and reasons why it comes; there is no right or wrong reason. For some it is a semi regular occurrence, until recently that was not the way it worked in my life. What matters not is the frequency, what I am concerned about is the fact that depression exists in the life of Christians and is not a sign of failure or lack of favour with God; I will come back to that.

My life was always one of change, as a child I attended 3 junior and 3 senior schools, lived in 8 houses in as many towns. Growing up in that way presents many challenges, not least of all finding new friends and trying to slot into their already settled existence.

I would say that church definitely helped inasmuch as it gave me a ready-made family in each new town; I never really struggled to make friends anyway and found church kids to be much more difficult to navigate than school friends. I generally got on better with the parents of my friends in church as I found the kids too boring.

It is a hereditary thing that I like my own company and would often just go off and play in my own little world if no friends were available. I quite like me as a general rule and could cope with being alone for a while before I would need outside input and interaction.

I have always been a thought-full person, by that I mean a thought can run around my head in a loop for hours if I don't check it. This can be a curse as much as a blessing, I have learned over the years to harness it when studying the Bible as it gives deep insights into verses and I see things I would otherwise miss. It's like taking the verse out and looking at it from every angle like a computer model. I believe that our brains are deliberately given to us with all of their quirks and nuances to perfectly suit the path we need to walk.

I regret nothing of my childhood, it was fun, rich and I know people all over the country, I know my way around Scotland without a map and could take you to places of interest, natural beauty and solitude (not all, some are just for me). If we can allow our history to be a pastor and our experiences to be a teacher nothing is a waste or a loss. Some experiences are horrible and dark but can teach us what not to do as much as how we do want to live in the world.

At a summer camp just before my twelfth birthday I came under the conviction of my sin and cried out God for Salvation. It was a quiet affair in the study of the preacher for the week, he was a gentle man who simply pointed me in the correct direction and stepped back to allow the Holy Spirit to work.

I was baptised three years later and began my Christian life in earnest; by this I mean that like most church kids in those days I was regular at all of services anyway. It was my life out with church that began to take on a completely different direction. I am thankful that God preserved me through teenage years without making any unwise or lasting choices.

When I was 16 I made a covenant with God to be His, by that I mean I offered my life to do and be whatever He chose. I have renewed that covenant many times after taking back the reigns for a bit; it has been hard to live what He has brought me to at times. When you hand your life choices over to somebody else you don't always necessarily agree with them immediately.

When I was 16 my parents moved abroad and left me to live in their house, initially my newly married sister and her husband shared it with me, but after a month spent visiting with my parents in the Caribbean I came home to a new job and a house to myself. I should point out that it was a two bedroomed flat in a local government estate, not some vast stately home.

Working in a new job on apprenticeship wages and running a home was incredibly tight; I was responsible for utility bills, house tax and food. I made financial decisions in those months that plagued me for years to come. During that time

I was ridiculously optimistic as most 17 year olds are, I loved my job and would speak about my faith with everyone at every opportunity, in church I was totally immersed and being given opportunities to preach a bit. I was devouring books and studying the Bible for the first time, in short I was pretty happy. I longed for a girl but who doesn't at that age.

By the time a year had passed my parents returned and I was changed completely, I was even more independent and insular than I had been before they left and was single minded and focused on learning as much as I could about God.

At the age of 21 I bought a flat of my own, I was nearing the end of my apprenticeship and needed my own space, my bedroom became too tight and I was always in there studying, if not at work or at church. Moving out was a quiet quick decision, not discussed with anyone. I just came home one evening from work, packed up and moved out the next day.

I loved the freedom and space of my own, my parents never did give me a curfew anyway but just to have the quietness and liberty was bliss. I had no TV and a large library, donated from deceased church members and living friends. In the days before Amazon and kindles, dusty old books were my best friends. I found that I had more in common with long dead preachers and missionaries than many of my contemporaries. I devoured Spurgeon, Lloyd Jones, Keith Green and countless other biographies while also studying through the New Testament epistles and increasingly preaching around central Scotland. I cried out to God continually to use me and He did.

A friend and I would go out on a Friday night at 10pm into the town where I lived at the time and we spoke to anyone who would listen to us about God. I loved it and prayed continually for the people I met. Results were never an issue, just speaking to them about their souls and leaving them to God was enough. It wasn't until I became results focused later in life that real problems began.

Early experiences

2

After finishing my training I was paid off, that was standard practice within the company. I then worked for 18 months in another job from which I also got paid off. I was then unemployed for 9 months. I applied for every job in all of the papers whether qualified or not, I was beyond penniless, the meagre amount assigned by the government to a single man was nowhere near enough to keep me afloat financially. That said, I never once doubted God was in it. Those years living alone were great times of finding out who God was. I began attending a Bible study in another town at a friend's house. We would meet after our own church study and just discuss what God was doing in our lives or teaching us at the time. I heard a friend begin to talk differently to anything I had ever heard before. He spoke of a personal communication with the Lord that would take us into His very heart. The whole concept was a revelation, I had always prayed but it was quite subjective and distant, this was totally different. I was discovering the Holy Spirit as a person rather than an 'it' as many people I was surrounded by referred to Him. The books that I was reading were opening my mind to new concepts and this Tuesday study was confirming what I was reading. We went to prayer meetings in one church and at one point the Holy Spirt started convicting the people there of their sin. The confessions and open hearted time that followed freaked the elders of the church so much that they closed it all down. Another time I was in my flat and was totally bored, I was lying on the floor begging God to use me when the door buzzer went. Standing there was a guy my age asking if I would give him a lift to collect his broken down car some miles up towards

Glasgow. I, of course, just went with it. We were driving mile after mile and no car was ever there, it was always 'just up here.' That is when your emotions kick in and I said that if he was going to steal the car there would be no resistance from me. He assured me that was not his intention. With that out of the way I blasted him with the Bible and we discussed it at some length until I realised that there was no car. He just wanted a ride to a friend's house (for a bag of drugs as it turned out later). I was a bit miffed but delighted to have the opportunity to speak to him. Over the next few weeks this was repeated and we became 'sort of' friends. I preached at him and he put up with it to get the ride to Glasgow. He never did make any sign of being interested but I let him have the full message at every opportunity, which never seemed to bother him much (sadly).

I also spent days with a Jehovah's Witness man when I was unemployed. He would come round every week with his colourfully printed arguments and verses of scripture. It started when two people came to the door and couldn't answer any of my questions; I had been studying their beliefs and was giving them a bit of a hard time so they called in the heavy armour. He was a lovely man and we got on really well apart from disagreeing on virtually everything in relation to scriptural interpretation and who Jesus was.

It was then that I applied for a job in Falkirk, 50 miles away. I had prayed about it and never got the job, I did get temporary work building computers in a factory over the Christmas period. 3 months later I replied to another advert with the same bus builders in Falkirk and had been praying that if I get the job I will move house as well. I got the job.

By this time I had been preaching very regularly in the group of churches that I was part of and was relatively well known, so my reputation for being a 'serious minded young man' preceded me. A friend had suggested that I could move in with her parents until I got my own place, so that's what happened. My flat in Kilmarnock was all but sold and it was looking very neat for moving on.

The sale fell through and I was left with a property nobody wanted. The area was deteriorating rapidly with the rise of hard drugs and the fact that they were freely available. The streets were awash with every pill and powder and the attending crime spree that invariably accompanies these things.

It was while staying with these friends in my new temporary accommodation that my first real bout of depression began, it was like a taster session. They had gone out for the evening and I was sitting alone listening to music in their comfortable lounge. This wave of darkness washed in like a towering tsunami, I completely sank under the gloom, my mind embroiled in the morass of dark thoughts about how hopeless everything was. I could see my new house being carried away in the wash of the Kilmarnock aftermath. This coupled with pinning my hopes on a girl from Wales whom I had been writing to for nearly a year (I know, I am that old) which came to an end. I sat there alone in the house my face buried in a plush cushion and just begged for God to end my life. None of these things in and of themselves were particularly hard but the hopelessness became unbearable and I just wanted out. Another good friend the next day tried her best to cheer me up with verses of Scripture but I was not receiving or interested. It was all just bouncing off the dark cloud in my mind. The aftermath of such waves is much the same as a tsunami, it takes a lot of clearing up before you can begin to build again, and thankfully this process has become easier with the passing of time.

That first bout passed in about week and it was all systems go again; I headed south for a weekend in Somerset with some friends and was spiritually uplifted. When I came home I rented a different flat and got on with life.

Not long after that I started going to a bible class for young people on a Friday night 20 miles away where I met my future wife, we got on great and always chatted. I was unsure in the extreme what she really thought (even with hindsight I confess that I couldn't have said unequivocally that I was sure) and never took a chance with her. It would be fair to say that I was very muddled about a lot of things in spite of being adamantly clear regarding others.

January 1998 was to be the next dip, I was so bad that church folks thought that I was ill or love sick. These were spiritual people, but at no time did anyone think that this could be a deeper issue. The darkness just clouded me day and night and I couldn't escape. I was fairly prone to taking things personally and found the situation in church quite difficult; there was a man being mistreated and I had to go after him when he ran out of the church after being badly spoken to. I hated seeing God's people treating each other in this way.

I mentioned earlier that my life took a change of direction during dark periods; it was during this time that the sense of finality became powerfully real. I was convinced that my life was over when in reality it was simply that this period of my life was coming to an end. I had continued talking to Fiona and was tortured about her; finally I gave God an ultimatum, if she was to be my wife she would agree to a date. I didn't want a girlfriend, I wanted a wife, and so if she said yes that was it and if she said no so be it.

The previous year I had spent eight weeks with a wonderful woman and was quite confused when without warning we both just realised that it was going nowhere long term.

At the end of February I was clear enough in my mind and asked her out: thankfully she said yes and we embarked on a crazy journey together.

I would love to say that I understood all of these things at the time of experiencing them, but it is only with years of further experience that I can see the progression of my illness and the timing of it in my Christian walk. So does God send these dark spells or is the devil attacking? Depending on who you speak to at what end of the church spectrum you will get many answers in support of both ideas. I have come to my own conclusions which in due course we will come to.

After a 7 month whirlwind we were married, that in itself was a story of my inexperience with women and what a proposal should be. It's a mercy that she is a Godly woman and saw beyond my gruff exterior into what my heart was like, even if I couldn't express it sufficiently at the time.

I had long held on to a dream of going to Japan, I had written to missionaries and read books about it for years. I won a sum of money in the Christmas draw at work which was more than enough for the ticket. That was just before the whole episode in the January. What then happened was a honeymoon, not to Japan but Ireland and I have never again wanted to go Japan or very much thought about it. I have experienced this time and again with the type of thought processes I have. An idea can become an obsession which is all consuming for a time and then once gone is seldom remembered. I am increasingly aware that this is common trait amongst minds like mine and unchecked can lead to more serious problems.

As a Christian I have a responsibility to control my mind and bring it into submission, Peter, Paul and most importantly Christ teach widely on this need. This is easier said than done when reason departs and logic is gone, when the broken houses and pummelled cars pile high atop the clear ground of lateral thought. Spiritual reasoning is lost during that time as the chemicals which normally regulate my brain are whirling like a hurricane, causing chaos within and without.

For the next 7 years we settled into church and married life, I was preaching and my wife was involved with kids work and toddler groups. We moved to a more open church and quickly became involved in many ministries. When our son was born Fiona took on the toddler group and saw it flourish. My own opportunities diminished as many of the churches I once preached in would no longer have me along any more. I settled into early 30's male pattern boredom, a dreadful malady in many churches that stifles and crushes thousands of men.

I still longed for more, in work I tried different jobs but still came back to being completely unfulfilled. I began a 2 year Bible study course in Edinburgh in late summer of 2006. It was an incredibly challenging course covering an Old and New Testament survey, Greek, Missions, Church history and various other topics. I had never enjoyed school or college but this really inspired me. I was getting grades in the 90% area which was an incredible buzz for me. I was glad of the distraction because the church went through an extremely difficult time and a survey was commissioned to see what people were feeling was wrong. I was asked to be part of the committee who were allocated a section of the congregation to visit and discuss a set of questions. I loved speaking with the people and quickly saw that there were huge untapped visions that easily rose to the surface with a few short questions. I was not alone in my boredom.

Illness progresses

3

I had began to sink in the January of 2007; the strain of the church situation and the feeling of emptiness crowded in and the dark cloud fell.

It was Fiona who thought of it first and asked if I thought I might be depressed. I took one of those online survey things and ticked all of the boxes. I also spoke to my Brother in law who is a doctor and he basically confirmed it. At that time I considered medication but a good friend who had been down that route put me off the idea saying that he found it greatly hampered his day to day functions.

It was a terrible dark time, I had no interest in anything, the children (by this time we had a daughter as well) were doing fine, our marriage was going well and work was undemanding. We had bought and were renovating a big old property which I was thoroughly enjoying and on the face of it there was no real reason for feeling this way.

The only stress was church. We desperately wanted to know what to do and were praying continually for direction. Outside of that I was simply existing, I remember standing at work begging God for a heart attack or something just to end the pain. He never answered that one! Well, not in the way I was asking Him to.

It was while I was going through all of this a work colleague spotted the symptoms in me and took me aside. He was the only one who truly spoke into my experience. He told me not to minimise how I felt and that it isn't a comparison thing, **your pain is your pain**, it's real, acknowledge it, own it, and find a way through. I sat one day in my managers office in floods of tears, I just was needing away from work but he was reluctant to let me go, he said that if I let you go home then you must promise to come back in tomorrow. He was genuinely worried about my mental and physical state.

I was still able to pray at that stage so pleaded with God for an answer, if He wasn't going to give me release at least help me through. The answer came in four sermons. I had been listening to a young preacher from Ireland who was part of the Vineyard group, he and his wife had started a church in the Causeway coast area of Ireland. He was from Glasgow and had gone over to start this work with his wife and a couple of others. The church had grown over a few years and he had preached a series called, 'When darkness falls.' It looked at depression from a clinical, historical and scriptural perspective.

For once it all began to make sense, he spoke about God's darkroom where He forms and implants vision into our lives in times of darkness like a photo developer used to do on to photo paper. It all made sense, I asked God to continue to imprint on to my heart what it was I was to learn. He did, the pain never lessened, the difficulty remained and it wasn't until April at the Easter service in our in laws church in Sheffield that the darkness broke.

Also at that time our whole church studied Rick Warren's book, "Purpose Driven Life." In us as a couple was awakened the need to make our lives count. This coupled with the vision God had implanted made us even more unsettled. The vision was simple, people matter, every single one; the Christian who has lost his way, the hurt, the broken, the lost, they all matter. We had asked God to let us see what He saw, the overwhelming weight of that request was immense and thankfully it never stayed on us. No man is able to live with that weight continually on them, only one did and he was called the Man of Sorrows.

Sadly for us after a lot of prayer we felt the need to move on spiritually and through a friend we became involved in a Pentecostal church which was to become home for nearly 5 years.

I had always been reading since teenage years about the baptism of the Holy Spirit and the gifts that some people seemed to be blessed with. I had prayed and pleaded with God to give me everything that I ever needed to do the work He had given me to do.

That prayer had been answered. I was always equipped to carry out the assignment on hand even although I was continually striving for more and in many ways missing what He was doing at the time. This is a lesson my wife has been trying in vain for our whole marriage to impress on me, enjoy now!

I can honestly say that I seldom have, that childlike losing of yourself in a moment has eluded me most of my adult life. There have been times in church and alone in God's presence that I never wanted to end. There have been times with the family that were so precious that I forgot time but in general my brain is constantly moving on to 'what next.'

During this period of our life we went on the most crazy rollercoaster ride. We had bought an old house years earlier and I had spent most waking hours outside of work renovating every corner of it. By this point it was about two thirds finished.

Not long after reading the "Purpose Driven Life" we really put it all out there before God and as a couple said 'yes.' Whatever the request or question was, yes would be the answer from us.

The first six months in the new church, for me, were amazing. I loved the music, the freedom, the totally different approach and the belief that anything could happen if we had faith, it was liberation. The problem, however, was that the expectation level was huge. In this group of churches everything is big and bigger and extravagant. Juggernauts of travelling ministries roll through with bluster and boldness, bragging about the tremendous blessing they experience every day. Money pours to them and everything is great 'Praise Gad' all the time.

For a striving soul like mine it opens up a can of worms and discontentment; in and of itself it's not a bad thing, if you're overriding nature is content, then having that stirred every now and then is necessary. But to live constantly in that state is to welcome turmoil into your soul.

We were exposed to teaching that was all new to us and gave us another aspect to our Christianity we hadn't previously known. Unfortunately we were also treated like we knew nothing, all the previous experience of God and years of learning His word were wiped away; a spiritual superiority was rampant as we were made to feel newly saved and treated as infants. We had gone there with open hearts to learn whatever we didn't know and add to our faith, little expecting we were starting from zero in the estimation of many.

One thing that has long bothered me about many biographies and Christian books (and I have read hundreds) was the airbrushing of negative experience from the lives of the successful teachers. Now, clearly this is not an exhaustive list of events in my own life and to list every discouragement would be wearisome, but there must be a balanced view. The Holy Spirit did this when recording the Biblical accounts and we are the poorer in our day because we don't get to hear of the struggle and the back story of when it all went wrong, when we acted in faith and it never quite worked out as we believed it would.

That is the story of my life in many ways; it is also the story of Moses, of Joseph, of Paul and John. They lived hard, difficult confusing lives. Moses leaves everything to go rescue God's people and on the way at the travel lodge the Lord tries to kill him, it takes his wife to figure out what's going on. He gets to Egypt and Pharaoh laughs him out of town, the people, after initially accepting him, then get angry and tell him to beat it, "you're making everything harder for us." Paul brings the gospel to cities and is beaten up and stoned, he writes to churches and they call him a pretend apostle with no authority as they read the Bible for the first time. He faces his final court appearances in Rome alone, abandoned by all who had walked with him.

The great and the good in the church today are féted by all, they zoom around in private jets and motorcades lunching with celebrities and signing autographs themselves while the 'ordinary' Christians slog away in hardship trying to make ends meet and figure out where it all went wrong.

It didn't go wrong!

The history of the church is one of slow slog, seldom is it a vast ingathering. It does sometimes happen, but the sweeping revivals quickly pass and we need to get down to the business of changing; changing habits and thought processes. Changing from worldly minds to heavenly minds and that process is a hard day to day slog. Going to work, paying bills raising families and becoming the bride that He came to win. My wife reminded me recently that this mess of a church in the world is being formed into a glorious bride that will be presented spotless to Him on that last day.

We live in fallen bodies in a fallen world, we will get the same illnesses as everyone else, we need to pay the same bills, obey the same laws but we are children of a different world and therein dwells the hope.

My personal experiences and joint ones as a married couple have been filled with highs and lows, times of real assurance in the will of God and periods of great confusion, unsure if I am actually even close to where I should be.

Seldom in the middle of an experience have I fully understood what was going on, most of the time we just hold on to what we know to be true of God from His word even if the circumstances look to be contradictory.

I wish someone had been this honest with me.
Life doesn't always fit with the clichéd verses
that people throw your way and it seems that
God will use any circumstance and many means
to teach us what we need to learn and become.
His children over the centuries have lived lives
that made little sense when measured against
the teaching of the 21st century church, where
personal purpose and fulfilment is the goal at
the expense of personal holiness and
communion with our Father. I put this interlude
in at this point because during this time of our
lives we were being bombarded with positive
living messages and 'all things are possible'
teaching. All things *are* possible, but the 'all
things' are subject to the conditions of the
Heavenly Kingdom, it has never been a blank
cheque

I know from experience now that God will take
us to extremes in every direction for a time in
order to imprint into our psyche a way of

thinking, and then when the lesson is over we settle back somewhere away from the edge of that extreme. I have lived this so many times with different doctrines and lessons. We are to walk a 'narrow' path, which means holding everything in balance. Something that is so very difficult to live in practice.

After the 'settling in' period of the new church experience our next phase of learning began. I had been praying for an area of the town and the intensity of it increased continually. God sent people to pray with me and we focused on the area to see what God would do.

I had an immense burden to see people saved and was praying about the direction of my life. I was 33 years old and hungry for God like never before. Through a series of direct challenges and lessons in obedience I was convinced that I should give up working to focus on what God would have me do.

I was the sole breadwinner, the kids were young and the house was unfinished.

Rewind a couple of years and I had been increasingly acting on whatever I believed God to be leading me to do (I should point out that we were in all of this together as a couple, sometimes I would be learning something and Fiona would catch up. On other occasions it would be me catching up). It started with simple things like giving to people out of total obedience not knowing anything of their circumstances, or visiting people unannounced because we believed we were being directed to do so. It built slowly from that as we were led along the path of listening from that point of saying 'yes'. On one occasion it was reversed when our car was written off. We had decided to wait until after the summer before looking for a car in order to save a little. A friend from church turned up one night saying he believed that God wanted us to have his spare car, he handed us the keys to a fully taxed and inspected vehicle, no conditions or strings attached. This would happen again three years later.

The lessons built and stretched us to the point where leaving work seemed like the only option. To step out of the materialistic carousel is not well received, family and friends were very sceptical. The church people never understood how it was sensible or possible to live like that but we did, for almost 4 years. Herein lies one of life's great contradictions; we preach messages on radical obedience, we tell people to engage fully with God and that everything is possible. When we then are confronted by people who respond to our preaching and come to us with something that is out of the ordinary we tell them that perhaps they misheard God. Of course it can't be a free for all but it takes wisdom in a leader to know where his people are in their walk with God.

We just lived. Some weeks there was plenty, some weeks we fed the family for £20. We always had food for the kids, we always clothed them and gave them little treats but it seemed impossible that we could live like that in a cash orientated society. I am not implying in any way it was all good, we had times of real deep questioning. We faced eviction for mortgage arrears only to have it paid at the last gasp. I sat under a hedge raging at God because we had no food in the house and no means to get any, only to return home to a £100 voucher lying behind the door. But what we learned of God in those years cannot be learned in a classroom. I learned how to be a human being, not a human doing. I learned how to love and see people as God sees them, when our house was robbed (while we were at church) our overriding feeling was sorrow for the desperation of the people who did it, and not loss over our own possessions. Only God could do that in us.

We sat with alcoholics on the street and just loved them, we took an asylum seeker in for a year, giving him food and shelter. Our house had a revolving door for everyone at any hour. Twice more we were guided to take in people for long periods of time. The kids loved it, they learned how to get on with anyone of any culture and status and are the more rounded individuals for it.

We learned about spiritual warfare and were privileged to see things that would have freaked us out previously.

A passion which had begun during my last bout of depression for people saw its outcome during those years. We had been praying for the wandering Christians of central Scotland.

One Sunday morning we had a clear direction to open our home and set a table of remembrance, I had said to one person during the week about it and on the Sunday there were 10 people there. For six months we did that and we saw about 25 different people come and go, 2 people were saved and baptised (one of whom was a friend of the alcoholic guy we spoke to who had turned his life around. We had decorated and furnished his flat and the love of God overwhelmed him) and when our time together had run its course they all went on to other churches.

I believe the end of a thing must be as clear as its beginning and to carry on beyond is to enter doing it in our own strength.

I had been hobbling around with a sore hip for a while and the consultant was trying everything to avoid operating on it, so I had injections, pain killers and ultrasound guided injections but nothing was working. I had people in the church pray for it and I became quite sure that an operation was the only answer. I believe that on occasions God will heal miraculously as we have seen it happen, when we prayed for a friend in our home who was relieved of her chronic back pain in an instant, but a skilled surgeon is to me as much of a miracle. That God can heal is not up for question, how he chooses to do so is up to Him.

In the last year before returning to work we had started a Bible study in our home at the request of several Christians, it began around the kitchen table but soon needed to move to the sitting room which can house 20 fairly comfortably. Again we started to see disaffected Christians rediscover who God is and grow strong as we studied Nehemiah together. We also prayed into the area of the town I had been challenged about and spoke a lot about helping people, which we did as opportunity presented itself. Over that year we saw a lot of people come and stay awhile before moving on, but around 15 formed a strong bond. I married my first couple that year from the study group.

I was scheduled to have an operation in the October and pushed myself after it to be upright and well enough to conduct the wedding. It was too much for my body. I mentioned the recent study about depression being linked to inflammation. The operation was huge, cutting through skin, tendons and muscle, he dislocated the hip and replaced it after cleaning away the calcification that had gathered. I pushed myself to be fit to walk within ten days, fuelled by determination and Tramadol I stood and danced the night away.

After the wedding I completely crashed and December was a black hole of unfeeling and hopelessness.

I spent that whole month in a darkened room watching the TV show Lost on box sets wishing that I was in Hawaii. I cancelled the Bible study and just hid. I remember standing in floods of tears talking to the girl staying with us at the time about the futility of it all and the uselessness of all we had done. She was desperately trying to reassure me but it was pointless. During that month the physical darkness in the room mirrored my mental and spiritual conditions, nothing was getting in and little was coming out. Knowing what I do now, my body was desperately trying to heal itself and the inflammation was affecting every part of my being, from the wound outwards.

Darkness lifts

4

The New Year brought new hope. I was feeling the need to get a job and began applying for work; my old workplace was employing but I didn't want to go back there. It is a really steady place to work but there isn't any place else that I have experienced that compares to it. 600 bored men passing the days until death with only weekends and holidays to look forward to. The gloom and malaise takes its toll on me after a while.

 I had said, somewhat petulantly, one morning while praying that if "You want me to go back there they need to call me." Within half an hour I had received a call from my old manager, so reluctantly I was back in the factory. The reverse culture shock was worse than I had imagined, it took me over six months to settle back in. However, I went to my old locker and my overalls were still hanging there with my name on them. It was like I had never left at all, in fact many people asked if I had been on the nightshift.

Suddenly everyone in our little study group was talking about starting a church in the housing estate that we had been praying for, we had been welcomed by the people we were helping and they were all passionate about having a Christian witness in the area. I had been praying around the area for 4 years by this point and somewhat reluctantly started making enquiries about a building to use.

We managed to secure the Community Hall to rent for a reasonable price and spent the month of February praying for the beginning of March as a start date.

It would be fair to say that my passion was always for the restoration of Christians and that preaching to the lost was something else that I always did as opportunity was there.

It's no surprise that from day one we started to see wandering Christians gathering as we preached through Haggai. On the week leading up to our first service one of our musicians had his shift changed and couldn't make it, on the Tuesday God saved a young man who was connected to the other musician. In his house, on his own the weight of God landed on him like a bag of coal and he was taken through his abject spiritual poverty and need of salvation. He played guitar on the Sunday.

Things went on really well, people were changed and grew spiritually, and we had opportunities to help others within the community with household items. We posted a billboard proclaiming 'hope' on the busiest road in town. At Christmas we handed out dozens of food hampers and had really incredible conversations with many people. We were able to buy a bed for a woman who was sleeping on the floor of her bedroom because she had no money to get one.

Our numbers had grown to about 25 and the Bible study carried on as well. We had every challenge imaginable in those days. Every condition that humans get themselves into by fault or just circumstance came our way and we just found a way to help them.

One of the men had been through rehab and was progressing really well until he was put on to methadone, we really lost him at that point but he lost his life when he slipped back in a moment of weakness. If the love of others could have saved him, he would still be alive today. Sadly I had to conduct my first funeral. As a self believing super hero it is incredibly difficult to admit that you cannot save everyone. Fervent praying and hours of investment into the lives of others does not always result in change. We are all individuals and as such are allowed to choose our day to day path, even when it is totally wrong.

In the January I had to go to the Home Office in Croydon, on the south side of London, with one of our men who was seeking asylum. His case had been ongoing for four years and we had been at every court right up to the Court of Session in Edinburgh. This court is the highest legal establishment in Scotland, they set legal precedents there rather than judge petty crimes. In actual fact his barrister won the case and a new law was written down that enables asylums cases on religious grounds to be reheard in lower courts. We drove down to London one evening in preparation for his appointment the following day. I dropped him at the Home Office at ten in the morning and waited all day to take him home. At 6pm I received a call to say that he was being detained and sent to the detention centre at Heathrow. I felt like my insides were being torn out, he had lived with us for almost two years and the kids called him uncle, and just like that, he was gone. I drove home in a daze and the next day we got on the case again. His lawyer was furious and asked how much we could gather together as bail bond money? By days end we had £1200, the lawyer was dumbfounded but secured his release. Within a month and one more hearing in Glasgow he was a UK citizen

I have long listened to preaching and read books relating to men and women of vision. I have studied the form that it takes in individuals lives, when God implants a vision for a time or a lifetime it is important to understand the context of it. It is also important to understand the timing of things. This was one of the key lessons we were taught over many years and in many situations. A vision can be given to a church or a person and sometimes the line between the two can get blurred. When Daniel got his vision in the Old Testament he was clearly told that some of it related to him and the nation of Israel while other parts were for many years in the future.

I am convinced that we will get a vision for something that God desires to do on earth. As Jesus taught His disciples to pray He told them to seek God's will to come to pass here on earth as it already was in heaven. Moses instructions for the tabernacle were specific requirements that were to be followed exactly because they were a pattern of something that was in the heavens.

The church pattern that Paul wrote of was something to be specifically followed because it represents an order of things that the angels are observing. All of that said, the first century churches failed in the pattern and many lasted no more than two generations. Does that mean this thing doesn't work? Since the creation of angels before time and the advent of mankind we have had constant rebellion from the perfect plan of God. This has led to misery and hardship, failure and sin. Whenever we bring people into any vision it has the potential for failure. However, we need to be of the mind that anything done under God's guidance and in His strength is never wasted.

After our second Christmas we had planned a music event in the local park for late April, it was to be a fun day with stalls from local businesses and community groups, but also to be a completely free event. Four years prior to this, a friend and I had been meeting to pray every morning for the area. One morning we went down to the park and prayed around it for about an hour. It was at this time that the seed was planted in my heart and the battle for the souls of the area began in earnest. A friend from America had been praying for Falkirk and wanted to see something done as a witness, as a result we received a cheque to be used in an outreach. This money funded the whole event; we hired a sound stage and five bands came to play over the three hours. A local friend preached about God's love for us in between and the singers testified about the work of God in song. The Fire Service came with a unit and made a dramatic exit at the end of the afternoon when a call came in. The local youth club gave us 3 inflatables and people to look after them. There were football games and the ice cream van came and parked next to the hot food man. Around 300 people came and witnessed a totally free event and heard about the love of God for them.

From that point on the church changed, there was no great dispute in question, nobody had fallen out but people left for one reason and another. So by the time the summer came around we had barely a dozen people remaining.

I would say that around the April I started to sink again, it was gradual at first, but by the summer it was getting bad. The stress of arranging the fun day whilst working full time, the weekly preaching and setting up of the hall and the care of each person took its inevitable toll. Our usual summer camping trip came around and I was barely functioning; I had no interest in fishing or much of anything, I was staring blankly in the sunshine with my hook not even in the water and not doing much else.

I had been preaching every Sunday and leading bible study for two and a half years. I was working full time as well and dealing with the church issues almost single handed, Fiona was always a support but most of the decisions and problems required my full involvement. As much as I had tried to delegate responsibility and bring others in to help, I had not been successful. I conducted two more weddings that year. The pressure involved was heavy and the slide down was slow but steady. After our holiday we discussed my condition and decided I should go to the doctor for help; by this time I couldn't even string a sentence together, I was unable to process or make a decision. What I needed was space, in my head the thoughts were constant and the pressure was huge which I placed myself under. I had returned to work but felt trapped and claustrophobic, I was getting panic attacks as well. The doctor prescribed anti-depressants and beta blockers for the crippling anxiety, she gave me a few weeks away from work to let them settle in. The first one just made me nauseated, the second lot knocked me out completely; I slept for a week.

 As they settled in the side effects weren't really that good so the doctor tried a third kind, this time they were great, no side effects but numbness of mind. I continued to preach after that until October. Quite how this was a good idea to me I will never know. Finally I was helped into a decision by a very good friend that I needed to have a complete break. So the church ceased that weekend.

With the benefit of hindsight I can trace back to the things that chiselled away at my mental health, things that should have been resolved as they happened instead of being pushed aside to make way for the next Issue. Had there been a team of leaders or responsible people to share in the burden and to pray together over all the different things that came our way it may not have weighed so heavily on me. It is easy now to see where it slowly unfurled like an old sweater and even from this side I am at a loss as to how I could have worked it differently with the group of people we had around us at the time.

What I do want to achieve in writing this is to acknowledge what it actually achieved in the lives of the many people we had the privilege of spending time with. We had always said that we were happy if people walked with us for a time and moved on to wherever God led them. In practice, when you are trying to reach a community and rely on the support of a small church, seeing people continually move on is very unsettling for a pastor trying to plan things. I believe that we had always the people we needed at any given time and a lot of my problems were self-inflicted as I have such crazy expectations of everything, especially myself.

I had started writing this by saying that depression in the church is much avoided and misunderstood. For the most part it is completely ignored or used as a guilt trip for a lack of faith. I have heard many preachers say that a Christian should never be depressed and if they are that it is a misunderstanding of who they are and what Christ has done for them. I would agree that there are many Christians who live in doubt and fear due to a lack of understanding, but a clinical disease is radically different from a spiritual misunderstanding.

I have read the Bible through every year for the last 20 years; I have studied and preached on most of the epistles and large swathes of the Old Testament. I have a long way to go in plumbing the depths of this incredible book and a lifetime won't suffice to get close to it. However, none of that helped when all reason departed. You get to know the difference between being down and discouraged, and full on depression.

My descent at that time was slow and imperceptible to me, but to my wife it was more obvious.

I became irritable at pointless things, I grew angry at life in general but focused it in on others. I withdrew slowly from my family and was drinking to block out the pain in my head. I have suffered from migraine headaches since early years but the mental pain of churning thoughts and repeated analysis of everything is a slow torture.

I started working even more hours because it gave me some escape and a little satisfaction to be in control of at least one area of life. I had convinced myself that I was ok in the run up to the summer but when I was isolated in a tent for a week with just Fiona and the kids it shone a deep light into the reality of my situation. Such was my mind that it took my wife to point out that which I couldn't see myself.

The second week of my holiday was taken up with sitting on the terrace in the sunshine and not much else. They say we should listen to our bodies and adjust our behaviour. I was forced to do so, rational thought departed completely. I had been renovating our old house for 11 years, as the money was available I would do some more. I tackled everything from plumbing, plastering, fitting the kitchen, windows and bathrooms, basically anything that needed done. At that point of my descent I couldn't even work out how to do the most basic of tasks, I literally couldn't figure out how to do things, even simple things were beyond my capabilities.

The miracle in all of this was every Sunday I was able to prepare and preach for nearly an hour.

The last few Sundays are interesting in that I was addressing myself really. I spoke about Elijah and Jonah and their mental struggling over the will of God. Specifically Elijah has been well used to illustrate what mental exhaustion in the work of God looks like. I could completely relate to him in that cave, probably blubbering and angry with God at how things had turned out. In actual fact he too was believing the lies that his mind was feeding him, he wasn't alone, he had not failed, he was simply exhausted.

I won't go over the doctor thing again, but between her and my supervisor the support was unsurpassed. Fiona was always a solid rock to me and was nothing but a help and support; she has been and is the most amazing person who ever walked into my life.

The three weeks I was signed off from work were a blur, I had left work early because of a panic attack and gone into the hills. I always think better out there but not at that time. It was while out there wandering in the sunshine that I concluded I needed medical intervention.

Both during the summer holidays and while I was off work the Sunday services were carried on in a reduced form of a time of prayer. Fiona had been doing the Sunday school and wanted to continue with that while there were still some interested children.

I would say that in the month of September just before we finished up, the only moments of light that I had were while preparing for and preaching on a Sunday.

Fiona also ran a week of children's club during September which was a resounding success, there were a good number of children came and heard about how God can change lives; it was the most bizarre of situations. I was a mental wreck, the numbers had diminished to a handful but I always had a message and the reputation we had in the community was amazing. My wife stepped up and followed her heart and in those closing few weeks she poured herself and her abilities into the children of the community.

I titled this book darkness in the Light because I have always I loved the idea that we are the light of the world, we walk in the light and are children of the light, our task is to let His light shine through us, and yet for months I was in complete mental darkness.

The more exuberant members of the churches would want to pray over me and cast out whatever demon was oppressing me, all the while telling me to up my faith levels. Fiona fielded more of these people than I will ever know, like a strong sea defence she has repelled and shielded me from a lot of external nonsense.

I have had periods like the great king David of crying out to God on certain subjects (as he did in the Psalm in our introduction) and hearing no answer, I have had periods of asking and receiving answers almost immediately. What about those who are in the middle of a period of no answers simply because there are no questions. Truthfully there are innumerable questions, but none which make any real sense to your logical self. The words which I would have offered others were of no help to me, the bridge to spiritual and mental reason is gone. Contrary to what many people believe Christianity is a reasonable faith. Countless times in his letters the Apostle Paul encouraged his readers to use their brains and logically think his teaching through. Depression robbed me of that capacity when the wave rolled in.

I had plenty of questions, none that anyone could answer though. When the children were little there was a programme on the kids channel that had the 'Why bird' as its centrally annoying character (why are they always so irritating Mr Why bird?) this bird lived up to its name and I turned into it (minus the blue plumage).

I had anger levels that I could barely control, I had inward Tourette's (I have never really been a swearing person, turns out that I know a lot) and the downward spiral just kept on going. I was angry at everybody and everything. I was angry at God most of all, why had it all come to this, to nothing. After all of the years of sacrifice, of struggling, of putting up with mountains of rubbish in various churches, this is what we were reduced to?

I sat at work and did just enough to get through the days not even able to listen to music of any kind. I have always loved music of every kind, I even taught myself to play the trumpet. But during that time I couldn't stand any music of any kind, Christian music made me laugh at its banality and I couldn't talk to anyone. Many days I begged God just to take me, just to end the mental torture and give me respite from the thoughts that churned around like a violent sea dredging up all the doubts about everything.

Ecclesiastes was the only book that made any sense to me, what was the point of anything? My house, that I have worked so hard to restore will pass to someone else soon, the pain and sacrifice of those last 8 years had come to nothing but me being a frazzled, burnt out shell of the man who I once was. All the people we had helped and hoped for were gone and it was like standing on an empty beach with the tide out. My phone, which used to ring and blip with texts continually, was silent and the doorbell never rang. "It was all meaningless and a sowing of the wind."

Falling into a cyclical pattern with these thoughts is like a slow poisoning the mind. I now realise that if I had been speaking to someone who was objective I may not have gone so low. That said, I had no desire to speak to anyone anyway, I just isolated myself from everyone out-with work and close family.

I did have one friend who would text regularly to make sure I was coping with life and not planning anything rash. He had a real concern for me, and I know he was praying a lot, so too were many others.

I met an old friend of mine for coffee on a semi regular basis and he understood that I just needed space and time, he has lived with this for many years.

I am not implying that no one ever showed any interest, it was just so stark in comparison to the frenetic pace and level of people we had around us for so many years. My sister in law was also a great communicator and showed real concern.

My hope is that if you have anyone in your life that is going through this horrendous darkness that you will just be their friend. No advice, no pressure, no comparisons. We don't care that there are other people way worse off than us, we don't care about very much of anything. The medication takes the edge off but isn't a magic pill, the thoughts are all still there. For me time was the only thing that helped, I process things slowly and imperceptibly, like a disc defragmenter on a desk top computer things slowly get put back in the correct place.

Unfortunately for the friends and family of people in this situation there is no one answer for how to help. I have been very fortunate to have an incredibly understanding and patient wife who allowed me to work through this process and gave me time away without demands. On Sundays she would take the children to a local church, to give them continuity, and give her sanity, while I would go have a coffee somewhere and either read or walk or just do very little but freewheel without any need to be anywhere.

Having spent a lot of time recently trying to make some sense of these events I wanted to open up my mind to see what was going on, the best way to describe how it went after that summer was like having a tornado in my head and in the dead zone of the middle of the tornado all sense of reason dropped like a stone and kept falling for months.

As a very driven person (normally) I have always been pushing myself to more and better in my spiritual life. I have not been out of a church environment for any more than a week or two in my whole life. So to spend 9 months in this wilderness of isolation was a very different experience. I had no desire for church or Christian company I had no desire after God or His things and it took until late December of that year for the anger and sense of disappointment to begin to subside.

I had been writing small articles as I was inspired to do so and it amazed me that in spite of everything else these times of inspiration and clarity were Bible based and Christ focused. In December I was impressed with a line from Silent Night about Love's pure light, and found that His light shone into the deep darkness of my mind even for such a brief day.

A brief respite

5

The turning point began at the end of December when I contacted a counselling service. The man completely understood where I was coming from. I should say that I felt the need of a Christian counsellor because of the nature of my situation. He was able to relate to the causes and circumstances of how things had come about. He gave the Martyn Lloyd Jones book referred to in the introduction which was straight talking and medically balanced with scriptural insight. I always responded to straight talking so this approach worked well for me, that is not to assume the same will work for everyone who is suffering under this illness. It is essential to get someone who understands where you are and how you tick.

The timing of this was also key, I was ready to speak to someone, my mind had healed sufficiently to allow me to begin processing through the complexities of how I had come to be where I was.

Depression is not a pretend problem, (we cannot simply "shake it off") not primarily a spiritual problem and now that it is proven to be linked to inflammation it must be treated accordingly by church leaders. I always said if you have a broken leg you don't sit and pray that it will get better, you get yourself down to the hospital and get a cast put on it. Why then do we treat mental illness as a purely spiritual problem? If this latest experience has taught me anything it is that my mind is a fragile organ and needs as much care as any other part of my body.

Talking through the basics of my circumstances enabled me to then begin to process what it had actually accomplished rather than my Ecclesiastes moments where everything was pointless and filled with futility. I referred earlier to the type of brain that I have been blessed with and how things can churn away in there like clothes in a dryer for hours and days. This thing that is such a curse when I am irrational is a huge blessing when it is centring on a positive outcome. So when I finally asked the Lord for help to see things as they really were, He graciously put them into an eternal perspective

I have already spoken about how I can now acknowledge and appreciate that this period we spent Hope Church was a time of great blessing and usefulness. I can see that we were privileged to spend time walking with some of

God's children and have the honour of speaking into their lives for a time.

When we ask God to 'use us' He does just that, these biblical characters we know so well were men and women just like us (James says so in his epistle). The whole halo circled picture that we have on stained glass windows was never the intention of their lives. We are nowhere asked to venerate them in the way that we have. I truly believe that they were people whom God used in their generation to accomplish His will on Earth and in every succeeding generation He has had His people that He could call on who were willing to just obey in spite of their weakness and sinfulness, recognising that God was able.

No matter what name that you pluck from the history of the church, they were great not because of who they were, or their education, or their position. They were great because of their appreciation of Christ and His calling on their lives. Most of the people from church history had personal issues, or quirks that would have seen them rejected from service by any review board today. But God always calls whom He will and sends willing hearts instead of 'qualified' ones.

I forget where it was I heard it but sacrifice has been defined as being, **"a huge risk with no guarantee of success."** That sums it up for me, I don't like that definition especially after having lived it. However, it won't stop me doing it all over again if the call comes once more. Now that I am returning to a measure of rationality, I can see these things as they truly are and not how I had been viewing them for so long.

I am incredibly grateful to those who have closed in during this darkest of times, they never gave up on me, they loved me unconditionally even when I was very unlovable and just believed that it was a *through*, not an end. I have read the glib statements like ' if He brings you to it, He'll bring you through it,' what if His '*through* it' is a walk through unfeeling darkness and hopelessness? What if *through* it are treatments that don't work, or life that ebbs away? Is that still ok with your theology?

Now that I am returning to the land of the living and beginning to have a hope for another future I can recognise that there is a lot of scar tissue that will need to be dealt with. When I had my operation those years ago I was not like an injured movie warrior who could stand and fight the next day. I couldn't even put my foot down for 3 days, walking was impossible without crutches. The wound was deep and the scar on my leg was tender for about a year, it is still pink five years on. Experiences like this that cause wounding and lead to depression run deep and the scar tissue is not the same as your original skin. It's softer, smoother and not as robust in many ways. I have never taken the time to examine and analyse the history of my illness before now and I see that I will need time to heal. I have begun the process, I am seeking out Christian fellowship and teaching. I see my deep need to be among worshippers to relearn what a privilege it is to do that and return to God what is rightfully His. These are early steps, what's the rush anyway? God isn't taken by surprise by anything we do, He has all the time in the universe to get us ready and finish what He started.

Over Christmas I decided to halve my medication as an experiment, it has gone ok so far, in fact in went so well that I have stopped taking the anti-depressants completely. I feel happy again, I am beginning to see reason and reality. Its early days still and I am going to push through this bit to see what the new me is to be. I didn't like that version of me, the one who was unresponsive and numb, who was hopeless and wrung out. The man who had no desire to be with anyone. This new version of me is yet to be directed to where and what but I am restoring my confidence with every line that I write. Can I encourage you as I am encouraging myself to remember the goodness of the Lord and what great things He has accomplished through you, in you because you said yes. This is not an exercise is justification or look what I have done, it is what He did in and through us. My counsellor has spoken about being 'wounded in the house of your friends,' the church is a scary place sometimes and the service of God is not for the faint hearted. He takes us higher, lower and further than seems logically possible or sensible, but He does see the whole picture of what each Christian will eternally look like. This hollowed shell that I have been was never the real me, I was still here but in a greatly reduced form. I was way back in the cave, far from the entrance looking out at real life passing by with no desire to get involved. People went about their lives as normal, sun and moon rose and sunk, days turned into months and my character was a pale watered-down version of the real me.

If anything in the church is going to change with regards to mental illness we need to stop seeing it as a weakness, or a failure or a purely spiritual problem. It isn't a reflection on our pastor, or our leaders, or our walk with God. All of these may contribute or hinder the process, but it is an illness. Some people get four colds a year, other people never get the cold, so we could list million illnesses but there are things we can do to minimise the possibility of getting sick. When they speak to the oldest person in the world (who changes a lot) they always ask what they attribute their long life to. One says, 'a glass of wine a day.' Another says 'I stayed single.' And the list goes on with each different person that they speak to. I can't prescribe an exact list for everyone as to how to live with or avoid depression, I can work out what the triggers are for me and set watchmen for them.

I hope in the future to be able to look for patterns in my life, as I have tried to do in this book, and watch for them surfacing in my life. I may get depressed again, I may not, it's a fickle illness that lies dormant in my normal life, rearing its gloomy head and clouding every part of mine.

The picture that I described to my friend was like a massive cloud, dark and looming over me and my life. I could see rays of sunshine at the edges of it, I could see other people living in the sun and enjoying it, but it was too far away to get to and to be honest the effort involved was too great. Breathing and eating were enough to handle at that time.

Life, for me is returning. Laughter and fun, being able to engage with the children and enjoy spending time with them. I can see that I have a way to go before I could consider engaging in any kind of meaningful service with God. In writing this I have relayed an account of my rollercoaster life in all of its many changes. I am also acutely aware that there is a coldness to me still, I get emotional at odd things in movies and on TV but when it comes to the things of God there is still a hardness that I am praying He will, again, remove.

I know that He will, He has done it so many times before. For now, as I read and pray and begin to return to church services I am trusting that the gentle 'still waters' will be the source of healing that this heart of mine requires.

Like I said, this was never supposed to be an exhaustive medical or spiritual consideration of depression. It is just my experience of descending to a place of darkness while being a child of the light. If it can help you to see that you are not a failure, or weird, or alone and help those around you to see you a little differently than they do, it may just have been worthwhile going through this last year.

The prelude was over

6

I wrote these previous pages at the start of 2015, since that time I have ridden something of a roller coaster of emotions.

The year rolled past without too much in the way of change, I was relatively stable although continued to self medicate with alcohol. As the summer rolled past and Autumn drew to a close we decided to look for a new church which we could attend as a family. After a futile search in our own town we decided to travel into Edinburgh to a church that was familiar to us. I had attended a Bible study course there some years before and continued to meet with the pastor once a year for coffee and catch up.

My confidence levels were fluctuating erratically at times and initially I turned the car around and went home. On week two it was better. From the start of November through to the following Easter we travelled each Sunday morning the forty five minutes into this thriving city centre church. The sound teaching and strong leadership was exactly what we were needing, after each service we would sit in Starbucks and enjoy a coffee as a family before heading home for dinner. These were good up building times.

By the time March was ebbing out the driving was becoming too much for me to cope with. Our heart was for our home town, not Edinburgh, much as we loved it.

Throughout those first three months of the year my thoughts were continually of ending my life. Day after day it was pretty much all that occupied my mind, like some morbid soundtrack that played over everything that we were doing, it never ceased. Finally I went to see my doctor again. As usual she was amazing and prescribed a low dosage of a completely different anti depressant. Within a matter of weeks things had begun to stabilise. The underlying darkness slowly melted away and life settled on to an even keel once more.

Not, however, before my anxiety kicked back in at work and I needed to be signed off again.

I was standing in my hallway one Sunday afternoon about that time desperate to have some Christian company, looking out of my study window the lights of the little church fifty feet away shone from their rear window. So I got ready and made my way over, I was very late. By the time I got there half of the service was over already but it was just enough to cope with. The welcome and the love I experienced that night convinced me that I should go back. These had been our neighbours for thirteen years and we knew them well, but for the first time I actually wanted to be with them.

Being off work gave me time to adjust to the new medication, it was warm and I pottered away in my garden and completed our greenhouse.

The next Sunday I went round in the morning and successfully lasted the whole service. There was an understanding that I received which drew me inexorably in, it didn't take too long for us to be going as a family. The safety of this little church group gently soothed us and its loving ministry calmed our damaged hearts.

I preached my first sermon for over two years just after the summer. It was like stepping out of a gloomy cave of isolation into the glorious blaze of summer sunshine. For forty minutes I wasn't ill any longer, I was alive again. The words flowed in glorious freedom and with astounding alacrity the pistons pumped thoughts and connections, illustrations and applications until I was done. The joy of those moments brought back all of the long dead feelings.

As ever, my amazing wife kept pushing me to betterment. She desperately wanted us to have the best life we could and so I contacted a local counselling service. During the summer I had been forced to face certain realities within my wider family. I had written another book in an attempt to recall areas of my life that were missing from my memory. This dragged up deeper rooted issues which I was forced to face head on. The counselling began right on the heels of this (the timing was perfect). We immediately hit it off.

Session one was a 'get to know you' thing, will be suited to each other and would I trust her with the deep things of my heart. The answer was yes.

Spending ten Mondays with someone who was not a Christian, who was a woman and was fifteen years on from me was not my first choice, but she was the correct person. Everybody is so different, she would be saying things that my wife had already said, the reiteration of them in a different voice embedded them in my psyche and they took root. If you need to spend time with a counsellor it is essential that you get on, that you trust them, that you are willing to be honest and that you listen. We laughed a lot...mostly at me and my foibles.

I preached a second time, this time I spoke specifically about my experience with depression. The response to my honesty was resounding, I am totally convinced that we must drop our masks of pretence and be willing to be gut wrenchingly honest with each other. Otherwise what we go through is wasted.

So, it is another year. Year four of this illness being present, where am I?

The journey continues

7

I am here!

I have often looked at people with dementia or Alzheimer's and wondered what was going on in there. My own grandmother ended her days shrouded in a fog of confusion. I visited her just before she died and saw a husk of the woman that had filled my life. She sat there, tiny, in her large chair in the care home unable to even form a whole word, that intake of breath which held the promise of speech only disappointed when a single sound died away to nothing. A gentle woman in most of her previous days, she was now filled with some untraceable rage for the uncouth swearing staff and she lashed out at them as they passed.

Having seen the outward ravages of this illness and also the pictures of MRI scans taken of such brains it is hard to comprehend the devastation in function and also the large dead areas inside the brain. We are a long way from understanding the genetic reasons why certain people experience this drastic attack from within. The same, however, could be said about most cancers.

But what of her spiritual life?

During my visit I quoted a favourite hymn to her and for a few moments she returned. She made eye contact and I called her gran, I said that she wasn't half as bad as she would have us believe.....and she grinned.

But she was.

Her brain was dying from the inside but somehow in that moment the real person trapped in the fragile little body shone out. I have seen videos of similar things when music is played to Alzheimer sufferers. A guitar was hung around a grey haired stammering woman, as her grandson encouraged her to play and sing she was transformed into a different person. For those few moments she was her true self once more.

We haven't even begun to understand our brains, they control everything. Perhaps we never will and never should know all of the complexities of such a wonderful organ. If science fiction is a thermometer of where we would like to go it is probably better left unknown

As I entered year four of this current experience it was with some small degree of betterment. I must quantify that statement by adding that I am not better! The man who crashed so spectacularly those years ago has not returned the passion and desire is absent, the drive, determination and joy is not here.

In its place there is a dull drudgery that marks most days. I have just returned to work from my second long absence this year; the tsunami broke over my mind with great force on two occasions this year leaving weeks of devastation and self destructive mess. The hopelessness returned and with it the gloom which shrouds our family home with edginess.

In the summer I purchased a 125cc scooter, it is a joyful little beast that can carry me to and from work with ease. On the days when I was at my worst I would jump on it and charge off into the hills with my camera to distract myself from the worst of the thoughts. On these trips I bombarded myself from within the helmet with music of many kinds in a bid to wash the internal streets clear of the debris lying in there. Most days this had the desired effect and I returned in a lighter frame of mind before the rest of the household returned from their day.

The medication is once more stabilised, the worst of the thoughts are past again and perhaps there is now going to be a period of settled calm. I think of the 'madness' of king Saul and have too much affinity with him, only the gentle strumming of David could calm his troubled mind. I see Nebuchadnezzar munching the grass those long years like a cow. His wife daily wondering how long he would be gone, one day his 'reason' returned to him and he once more ascended the throne a different man.

In these moments where I have a sound mind I understand that this is not an ending of my life. This is a time of 'passing through' in order to change me from the person that I have been into the man who God needs me to be going forward. My times of 'grass eating' are horrendously difficult, both for me and for my close family. I still don't see what these times achieve yet, but I must believe that there is a reason for them. I cannot succumb to thoughts of random chance or pointless existence because my heart knows differently.

Our precious twenty first century minds rankle at the thought that these things could not only be allowed by God, but actually sent by Him.

Read again Daniel chapter 4, "**this is what is decreed for you**," in order to humble the mighty potentate and teach him to worship God he was sent to the fields for a time. Did he have moments of clarity in those years? Were there moments when the rain was pounding down on his exposed back, or when the noonday sun made his once pampered skin like leather that he 'knew.' Only he will ever know.

Or perhaps 1Samuel 16 where "an evil spirit from the Lord" would sweep over king Saul. Only the quiet harp and voice of the Spirit filled David would bring relief, on occasions even this wouldn't help and vitriol would spew from the king followed by whatever came closest to his hand to launch. Even Jonathon challenged his father's unreasonable actions and obsessional hounding of his once favourite captain.

I relate to these men in more ways than I would like to, on the worst of days of my illness there is no sense of reason, there is no logic and spiritual thoughts are unknown to me.

Every day as she left for work in these difficult weeks and I was wrapped like an enchilada in the duvet Fiona would say, "don't believe the lies." That was the best she could do, it was the best she could have done, no great inspirational quotes would have worked. No sweeping sermons or guilt trips would do it, no comparisons with slum dwellers or homeless alcoholics would matter. To someone who doesn't care to live or die it was the best advice a wife could give, and she understood that!

Today, with the understanding and clarity that behind every unhealed illness there is a purpose, that a loving Father has allowed this for my 'good' I should embrace the darkness rather than hate it.

But I do hate it, I hate what it has done to our marriage, I hate who I become in the midst of it and I hate the effect that it has on our home. For now, there is to be no permanent relief. Even if for a few weeks or months it recedes it is constantly there, ever lurking in the background with it's hot rancid breath never far away, leaving the lingering stench of loss.

Those 'privileged' few, who skip around the globe in their apparent freedom with bronzed skin and bling, flitting from yacht to Bentley as they dine on white sands at sunset are not the norm. They make for good magazine articles or slick Instagram shots but are children of a different father.

Yes, my own heart longs for such a life on occasions when all is going south, but even as I see them in those moments I quickly flip to the pointlessness of it all.

I still struggle to comprehend or understand dementia and Alzheimer's disease, but I equally struggle with every end of life illness. Our bodies will all slowly shut down one by one and it is we who differentiate between the mental and physical. Ultimately it is all physical, whether the damaged cells are in our heart or brain, it is all physical.

Was my grandmother lucid in those final years but trapped in a malfunctioning body? We won't ever know, but in those dark days which I myself experience I do know that I am being held to ransom by my own brain. Vital connections are not being made, the invisible prison bars are stronger than steel and the indoctrination that spews from the internal speakers is as powerful as any Communist re-education.

When all is said and done in these lives it will only be the spiritual 'me' who goes on, and that real person is who God is really interested in changing because I am eternal, as God Himself is.

How low can you go?

8

I am keenly aware that this book could be updated every year or so but since writing the last chapter a further two and a half years have slipped away.

Just after writing the last chapter everything collapsed once more into the deepest hole imaginable.

The stability that I was finding at that point was incredibly short lived and violently interrupted by an anxiety attack, the likes of which I have never known. I was prescribed Valium to settle things down and spent Christmas in a complete haze.

I was becoming increasingly erratic and angry at my lack of progress. My employer sent me for an evaluation with a psychologist who recommended 12 sessions. Unfortunately this was not covered by their health insurance so I was given a diagnosis with no access to the cure. If we had money to throw at it I could have seen a private therapist immediately but this not being an option I was added to a waiting list.

My frustration became unbearable with everything going on and the lack of meaningful support to help me move forward. As a couple we had been researching dietary change as a means to boost recovery and I completely changed what I was eating.

A combination of fruit, chia seeds, linseeds, turmeric and oily fish became my daily staple with a home cooked meal at dinner. The added bonus was steady weight loss, ironically the medication piled on pounds which only served to exacerbate the self-esteem issues.

The suicidal thoughts never abated in their intensity and I spent every day with that as a rolling mind-set. Each of these things are wearing on their own but compounded together they make for a harrowing existence.

Three times within six months the crisis team sat in our living room with the same advice:

- Keep an emergency contact number close by.
- Allow yourself no access to fulfilling the suicidal ideations.
- Keep close friends and family in the loop of your thoughts.

These are all great ideas in theory and I became further frustrated that none of these well intentioned professionals had ever had such thoughts.

The internal monologue of those darkest months was one of self-flagellation, hopeless pain and a constant gloom.

Imagine living with a murderer who repeats minute by minute what he will do to you, why you are worthy of his berating and constantly threatens to carry out his worst. Now imagine that this is inside your head day and night because it is your own mind.

No let up for months at a time.

You have been given a diagnosis, a sticking plaster is applied and you are dismissed.

I was sent home on numerous occasions from work because I was a danger to myself. I was cutting and scratching my arms, hitting myself with heavy objects, inhaling noxious substances, smoking heavily and drinking excessively even at work.

When you only want to die nothing is a threat, health and safety is a joke.

I desperately wanted help. I pleaded with the doctor, the crisis team and HR department to help me. They all said psychiatry was not the answer and I needed psychological help but offered none.

I persevered with life only because I didn't want to hurt my family, but I was living in a horror movie with an audience of one.

My thought life was horrendous at that time and I decided that what I needed was a drunken escape. I arranged to visit my sister and loaded up with much red wine.

I had a blast. Bertrand Russel describes drunkenness as temporary suicide, and it is just that. To get a brief respite from your pain is bliss. But you sober up, he continues, "the happiness that it brings is merely negative, a momentary cessation of unhappiness."

On the Sunday I had promised to visit the church of my Pastor friend, I was craving a bacon roll and Burger King furnished me with the answer. As I was turning into the road to the church an elderly gentleman ran the junction and spun my car. I watched with unbelief as my untouched bacon roll left my hand and disappeared somewhere to my right.

The consuming thought whilst exchanging details was where my bacon roll was, there was no thought of the danger or if the car was driveable. It was, I recovered my breakfast from the door pocket and went on to church.

Now bear in mind that I was still heavily drugged with anti-depressants, had spent two days drinking and was very tired.

I never mentioned anything to my friend and while sitting in the service I was even concocting a sermon if he had asked me to contribute (which did often happen).

When I left the church I drove on to my favourite beach on the North coast to gather myself before the drive home.

Anti-depressants are weird, you enter this other worldly state where everything is semi-suspended. Your own reality is all that there is and nobody else's situation really figures into it. I had just survived a major trauma, the car would be classed a total loss by the insurers and I was sitting on a beach enjoying a cigar.

I did have the foresight to visit my nurse friend for a quick check over before driving the three hours home. I called Fiona and was perfectly content that she should accept what had happened. I sent a couple of pictures of the car to reassure her and off I trotted.

The depressed mind is an inherently selfish place, I had no thought about how all of this would be affecting Fiona. Seldom during these times did I ever consider her trauma, her loss, her perseverance or her well-being. I never knew that she would rush into the house ahead of the children in case I was hanging from the loft. Or that she had countless anxious hours wondering why I was late or where I might be lying dead.

Decisions were made.

9

Two weeks after returning home I made a decision.

The anti-depressants were not doing me any good at all. I was at work and the side effects of the medication was driving me crazy; I was

- Agitated
- Anxious
- Angry
- Constantly tired
- My feet twitched incessantly.

The doctor prescribed an anti-psychotic to help with these issues. I returned to work and was an hour into overtime when the wave of hopelessness washed over me once more. On previous occasions I had contacted the suicide helplines and would text for hours with a faceless counsellor who defused the ticking time bomb. But on that day I was done, nobody seemed to be listening to my pain. The psychologist I had spoken to through my employer recommended 12 weeks of counselling but my healthcare didn't cover it. The NHS had a 12 month waiting list and it was too far out of my reach.

In a moment of complete calm I swallowed the entire bottle of pills that were in my pocket.

By the time we were eating dinner together I had all the symptoms of a heart attack and Fiona called an ambulance. They hooked me up to all manner of machines and whisked me away to the ER. It wasn't until I was speaking with the consultant that he asked some pointed questions. I still had the empty bottle in my pocket and gave it to him.

By this time I was hallucinating and was laughing. Thankfully the damage was not lasting.

After a day in the ward and a further psych consultation I was released. It never registered with me that it was my niece who picked me up and took me home. She had come to Fiona's assistance and as a senior mental health nurse was tremendous in her advice and support.

The amount of pressure on Fiona at this time was immense. Her family were excellent in their support for her but to be holding everything together at home and with the children was increasingly difficult. I was erratic in my behaviour and she never knew what she was coming home to face.

Living with this constant pressure, while trying to maintain a peaceful home and good environment for the children was pushing her to breaking point. So to have me away in a safe place for a bit in professional care was welcome relief.

Once again I was on sick leave being classed as a danger to myself in a factory environment.

Rationale was not present in those days but in my still altered condition I decided to abandon all medication. If I was capable of such drastic decisions while on the medication I reasoned that my brain wasn't coping with the drugs.

Ten days of withdrawal followed, everything from shakes to vomiting and wild sweating. I wanted to be free, to be clean and well. Emerging out of that haze was like floating to the surface after lying on the floor of the swimming pool.

The weather was unseasonably warm and I lazed around in the garden. About a month later I was swamped once more and started having panic attacks which led to another visit from the crisis team. He promised that he would fast track the psychology and left.

There was no fast track.

While I was off work I attended a men's conference. The overall topic of the day was around depression and seeking help with various different organisations taking part. Throughout the day I had this sense that I had to contribute something but largely dismissed it. By the time the evening session came around I was standing singing with the worship band and the organiser (who is a good friend) tapped me on the shoulder. He said that I would be taking the session. I knew exactly what I would be saying.

While driving north on my fateful weekend there was a BeeGees song that kept coming on from my playlist which basically asked "how can you mend this broken man and make him live again?"

The answer that I received was from Genesis where it says That "God breathed into Adam the breath of life." I was acutely aware that I needed God to revive me and that it was only Him who could bring me from the darkness.

I spoke bluntly about my depression, my suicide attempt and the pain of the last four years. Some men left because it was too raw, but many others were helped and thanked me for my candour. It still amazes me that even in the midst of such chaos there were moments of great blessing.

In May of that year I convinced the work's doctor that I was fit to return to work and reluctantly the HR department allowed me to return. Work was a welcome distraction, just to have people around me who didn't treat me as an invalid did help immensely and the dark humour of a factory environment was very fitting for where I was at that time.

In the summer we had a week in Spain. I was determined to get better, I purchased Joyce Meyer's book 'Battlefield of the Mind' and worked my way through it asking God to heal my mind.

I was still drinking too much, the free bar on holiday didn't help matters but the sunshine and heat brought a measure of healing. I began to see, through reading the book, the damage I had done to my family with my behaviour and there was some real progress, and many tears.

My niece spent some time with me in those weeks after returning and was the first person ever to say that anti-depressants were not designed for long term use. The initial purpose was to dull the immediate damage while other therapies were supposed to then rectify the roots of the problem.

About this time I read about a book which had been published regarding inflammation and depression. 'The inflamed mind' by Edward Bulmore was the result of his lifetime in psychiatry and recent studies into the effects of inflammation on depression. There have been many concurrent studies going on in the UK in various universities into these links and they are all producing similar results.

This book described me exactly, the white blood cells attacking the damaged tissue to repair it in the same way that they would flood into a wound to kill the infection and heal a tear in the flesh. The unfortunate thing about this system is that they attack somewhat indiscriminately, by that I mean that when a wound is healed we are left with scar tissue.

When this is going on in an inflamed brain they are also attacking healthy brain tissue. As a result of this my memory of those five years is very sketchy, there are whole events, people, and memories that simply no longer exist. Even now I find myself stumbling over words and forgetting basic things that seem just out of reach.

The study further identified in the test subjects that many of the people involved had experienced some childhood trauma. They noted that the undeveloped brain cannot process these events and often buries them. They further noted that a further trauma in adulthood can trigger theses buried memories and often results in depression.

A major operation, for example, fills the body with healing blood cells that cause major inflammation. They found that quite often during the recovery period people who were never prone to depression will experience it in some form.

This was my experience as I mentioned in chapter 3.

The mental exhaustion surrounding collapse of the church and all of the spiritual trauma attendant with it triggered my brain into the spiral downwards. I will address the issue that surfaced in the next chapter but before this all happened I had a dream.

I was going into Edinburgh with friends from work and had wakened up in a strange basement of a tenement building. I was without wallet, phone or memory. I called Fiona from a phone box and asked if she come and get me, she agreed but asked that it be in a neutral place. This seemed extremely odd but we agreed upon a supermarket café in Nairn on the North coast. She came in and was a bit nervous but behind her I could see my two children only they weren't children any more. They were the age that they are now and I had missed the whole intervening five years.

I woke up from that dream really troubled but had no point of reference for it.

Several times in my life I have had such warning dreams. It seems that I am blessed to have some degree of fore warning about things.

This doesn't help and we will never recover the lost years. It doesn't make up for the shell of a man Fiona and the kids lived with during that time.

Fiona called me the "Hollow man."

Towards the end of the year I began to think a lot about King Nebuchadnezzar. For those years that he was out in the field living like an animal with nails like talons, hair growing unhindered and eating grass, he was unaware of anyone else. I wondered if he had moment where he knew, if he had times where he looked back to the city and his life but was unable to do anything about it?

I also wondered if his wife stood on the palace roof looking out into the wilderness where her husband growled and snarled, wondering if she would ever get her man back. Her wealth and privilege was of no use to her while her husband was not there to be with her. Did she, like Fiona have an understanding that this was not terminal?

Early on Fiona had sought God for a promise, she did receive an answer that I would return, that we would walk through this and that the gait of our walk would be different.

If she had followed the advice of well-meaning Christians, books and blogs I would not have a wife today. Everybody told her it was a lost cause and that there was no betterment.

We need to do better, we need to encourage our sick, to encourage their wives and husbands that there is a way through. We need a higher vision than is offered by the common word of man.

An ugly truth and a way through

10

2018 went out in a haze of Valium.

Everything had been going along fairly well until mid-September when the mundane nature of my job began to wear me down. I pushed myself on for another few weeks but found the anxiety levels begin to escalate once more.

I finally succumbed and went to my doctor again in an extremely agitated state. She suggested a short run of anti-depressants but I refused. A lot of people don't understand that it takes around four weeks for the medication to settle into your system. These four weeks are not good, you get extremes of temperature, mood swings, suicidal ideations and terrible dreams. These were my symptoms but everyone experiences something completely different, or none at all.

We agreed instead that a short course of Valium would be a better option. This was a tremendous help, everything just slows right down. From the outside you look like a zombie and sleep a lot but from the inside it is a fairly pleasant experience. The anxiety just melts away.

When February came around there was phone call from the Psychology department in our town. I had been on the waiting list for fourteen months but was, by this time, in a fairly good frame of mind.

I immediately hit it off with the psychologist. She was an ex-Military police officer and had majored in treating soldiers with PTSD. On top of this her best friend growing up had gone along to a brethren church so she understood my background very well.

I had rejected CBT (Cognitive behavioural therapy) as a method of treating depression because it was all computer based and a solitary exercise. This did not suit me at all as I function much better in a dialogue based environment. The government funded and recommended approach to psychology is completely CBT based.

I definitely gave this woman a run for her money. It took quite a while and several attempts from different approaches before I locked in to the method that she was trying to teach me.

Part of the problem with prescribed methods whether they are psychological or pharmaceutical is that there is not a panacea. I was blessed on both fronts to have medical professionals who tailored their treatments to suit my particular quirks. Not everyone is so fortunate.

The basis of CBT is a fairly simple one, there is a cycle of thoughts, feelings and behaviours that perpetually feed in to one another in our minds and all have the potential to go in a cyclical motion all day. This traps us in a never ending spiral which can hold us prisoner all of our lives.

I said at the outset that I am a thought full person, so when a negative thought or memory would get into this pattern it could drive me nearly insane. CBT teaches us to break that cycle by identifying one of these things and changing it.

Writing to the early church the Apostle Paul said in 2 Corinthians 10:5 that we are "to take every thought captive, bringing it into submission to Christ."

I have preached on this passage many times but found myself being taught the principle by a secular doctor. She taught me to write down the times where I would drift into this habit and identify what had caused me to head off down the road. By journaling it I was able through time to identify patterns of thinking and trace them back to their triggers. By doing this you can then stop the process earlier and earlier until you don't get past the trigger.

During my darkest time there was a memory which popped like a cork to the surface of my black lake.

As a sixteen year old I was put in into a very compromised position by a trusted relative and controlled in a sexual manner. This was something that had made me very uncomfortable at the time but was framed in such a way as to be perfectly normal.

It wasn't until my son reached the same age that it dawned on me just how awful the whole thing was. My relationship with the person was deeply affected and had never recovered in the years following but they did remain in my life. Every time I was in their company I reverted to a childlike state and my wife could never understand what was going on.

This buried trauma was one of the things that required to be dealt with as the psychologist identified the continuing ripples of it into my early forties. I am not one of those people who looked for people to blame for my failings but this issue had long reaching implications on my teenage mind.

I should point out that the memory came back before I ever spoke to a counsellor. I had recognised that there was a period of my life leading up to the event that I had sketchy memories of. It was a very stressful time in our family all round and I forced myself to remember all of the details of those years.

Thomas Wolfe wrote a semi auto biographical novel called "Look Homeward Angel" which I had been reading. I decided to do a similar thing in order to pull out of my brain those faded years. Starting from last strong memory I worked forward until I came to the event in question. What had passed at the time as an uncomfortable experience crashed like juggernaught into my life with the full force.

Over the course of 2019 my psychologist taught me over and over the principles of breaking these cycles. She was very patient and helped to break in to my ruminating mind and to stop the perpetual cycle.

Add into this the thoughts of Eckhart Tolle in his book, "The power of now" and I began to see the invasive power of thoughts that had continually dragged me in to a cesspool of destructive thinking.

Our minds are incredibly powerful, they work all day and night keeping everything moving, pumping and breathing. They are the essential "us" that processor which enables us to function without ever realising it. But unchecked the myriad of thoughts that pass through our minds in a day can become destructive.

I learned that a thought is just that, it does not define who I am and can feed in to the predisposition of my nature. If I am naturally morose or gloomy these thoughts can magnify the weaker aspects of my nature. Left unchecked they can destroy me.

Gradually over the year I learned to identify the invaders in my mind and separate them from who I actually am. For nearly six years I had allowed my mind to freewheel into a place of destruction. All day every day I was assaulted with the thought that I was useless and had no purpose, so why should I live a moment longer.

All day I had images of destruction, suicide and anxiety. All day I possessed with the thought that I should end my life because it was hurtful, damaging, damaged and had no point to it.

Eckhart Tolle talks about the 'pain body' that most people hold within themselves. Every single thing that comes into our lives has the potential to add to this body. We view our lives through the filter of this entity and interpret people's actions and words through the lens of this body.

Once I recognised what he was talking about I was able (with the help of my psychologist) to unpick the root of my filter. It is essential to realise that this 'pain body' is not me; the thoughts that it produces are not me. Like the great apostle Paul said we are to filter our thoughts.

Finding this tool changed my life.

I do not owe this hurt anything. I gave it too many years and when I finally saw it for what it was the weight of it was destroyed. After this when thoughts would arise I could see them, identify them, acknowledge them and let them go without succumbing under their influence.

In the years of my deepest darkness I would practice mindfulness. I resisted this as well initially but gradually began to see the benefits of it. At lunchtimes when everything was quiet in the factory I would lie with my eyes closed and just listen. I could hear the roof creaking, birds outside, men laughing and in those moments peace would return.

Over the years I grabbed at anything which would give a little relief, not everything was helpful or even sensible but for those moments it gave a small hiatus from the incessant gloom.

As 2019 was drawing to a close my wife had begun to pray that I would get a meaningful job, that I would find a reason to be.

Towards the end of November I was making considerable progress. The psychologist was increasingly leaving longer spaces between our appointments and life was beginning to have a measure of stability.

I should point out that I still had anxiety attacks and instead of looking to Valium to calm them I would suck on a CBD lollipop. This calmed my anxiety in the immediate and taking these thoughts captive would stop the process as I could once more think rationally.

I listened to Eckhart Tolle reading his book on repeat and this gradually entered my psyche in a real way, so much so that by Christmas I was like a different person.

The freedom from the darkness and anxiety allowed me to have the clarity to seek God again in a meaningful way. I could see that there were many people who spoke negativity in my circle and I saw the need to surround myself with people of vision and hope.

At work everything was negative. There was no meaning to what I was doing and the hours were long. I had begun at the summer to explore outside work to fill the void. This opened up in an opportunity to use my skills in property maintenance. So I would be out several evenings in the week for an hour or so working in people's houses.

The difference that this made to my mental wellbeing was tangible; I looked for greater opportunities in this direction with the aim of leaving my job permanently.

A new dawn

11

In January of this year we made the decision to look for a new spiritual home. We had drawn up a list of local churches to visit with a view to moving forward as a family into a new chapter.

The first church that we visited was as far as we got. Everything about it spoke of hope, vision and a place to call home. I was still very cynical in many ways but found something stirring within me that had long been dormant.

Like the great king Nebuchadnezzar I looked up from my wilderness and felt life returning to my weary soul.

Out of nowhere I was offered a job in the sector I had hoped to one day to find employment. It seemed unreal, I had long thought that I was forgotten, that there was no way I could ever escape the dead end job I found myself in. But here I was, taking a leap into the unknown. Leaving a secure job with countless benefits on paper, but a death sentence to my mental health, into a self-employed position with prospects but little in the way of security.

It is now June 2020.

An old preacher I grew up listening to used to say, "we are immortal until God has finished using us."

I think that this is half of the story. Paul says that we are being

 "transformed into His image."

Until both of these things are true of a Christian I believe that we will remain here on this earth. I have not hidden my attempts to counteract this and take matters into my own hands when life became unbearable for me. Looking back at that time from a place of wellness I don't even recognize that man. I can still feel the hopelessness, the desperation and the pain of those years but the raw edge has dissipated. I am glad that I have this permanent record to remind me and it is my hope that the lessons learned will be a benefit to others.

There are many factors involved in all that I have recorded throughout this journey. This is my own particular experience with depression, with treatments, with failures and ultimately the goodness of God.

There are many songs in the Christian world just now that are ministering to me,

He is healing my spirit in ways that are astounding and I found myself on several occasions over these last six months just overcome with His goodness.

I was working alone in a house with my music on and the song, "God You're so good" came on, as I knelt on the floor, paintbrush in hand, I just wept with gratitude as His overwhelming goodness swept over me.

I am working with a group of men who want to talk about God's word and we discuss on a daily basis things that we reading and thinking about.

Last Sunday was father's day. As I sat on my roof terrace enjoying the evening sunshine I was overcome with God's goodness to us as a family. The world was in lockdown and yet as a family we have flourished, each of us in our own way have been largely unaffected by it. We have been blessed.

As I bring this to a close my final reflections are on something Fiona said to me on many occasions over the last six years. Sometimes I inwardly swore at her for saying it, other times it fell on deaf ears but still she stuck by it.

Romans 8:28

"And we know that God works all things together for good to those who love Him – who are called according to His purpose."

She would say this over and over to me, God is good, this is the goodness of God, God only does good.

When I first heard the song "Good good Father," I wasn't in a very receptive place, but looking back from this viewpoint I can see that He has healed me. He has stirred my deepest recesses and brought to light things that were long buried in order to heal them.

I will never look upon this experience with joy, it was horrendous in every way. I will however

look back in gratitude that He has brought us
through this fire and we are indeed different.

Lightning Source UK Ltd.
Milton Keynes UK
UKHW011456250522
403506UK00005B/548